20th Century
PERSPECTIVES

The Russian Revolution

Tony Allan

Heinemann Library
Chicago, Illinois

© 2003 Reed Educational & Professional Publishing
Published by Heinemann Library,
an imprint of Reed Educational & Professional Publishing,
Chicago, Illinois

Customer Service 888-454-2279

Visit our website at www.heinemannlibrary.com

Produced for Heinemann Library by Discovery Books
Designed by Ian Winton
Consultant: Martyn Rady of the School of Slavonic & East European Studies
Originated by Dot Gradations
Printed by Wing King Tong in Hong Kong

07 06 05 04 03
10 9 8 7 6 5 4 3 2 1

Library of Congress Cataloging-in-Publication Data
Allan, Tony, 1946-
  The Russian Revolution / Tony Allan.
     v. cm. -- (20th-century perspectives)
Includes bibliographical references and index.
Contents: What was the Russian Revolution? -- Russia under the czars --
The revolutionaries -- Lenin -- The gathering storm -- Bloody Sunday --
The October manifesto -- The coming of World War I -- The shadow of
Rasputin -- 1917: the first revolution -- The democratic experiment --
The Bolshevik takeover -- Building socialism -- The fate of the Romanovs
-- Civil war: Reds versus Whites -- Victory for the revolution -- The
last of Lenin -- Russia and the outside world -- The Soviet collapse --
The legacy of the Russian Revolution -- Time line.
  ISBN 1-40340-151-9
  1. Soviet Union--History--Revolution, 1917-1921--Juvenile literature.
[1. Soviet Union--History--Revolution, 1917-1921.] I. Title. II.
Series.
  DK265 .A593 2003
  947.084'1--dc21
                           2002004353

Acknowledgments
The author and publishers are grateful to the following for permission to reproduce copyright material:
pp. 5, 13 Mary Evans; p. 40 Hulton Getty; pp. 41, 42, 43 Popperfoto. All other pictures reproduced with permission of David King Collection.

Cover photograph reproduced with permission of David King Collection. On the cover of this book, Vladimir Lenin is shown giving a speech to Russian soldiers in Moscow on May 5, 1920.

Every effort has been made to contact copyright holders of any material reproduced in this book. Any omissions will be rectified in subsequent printings if notice is given to the publisher.

Some words are shown in bold, **like this.** You can find out what they mean by looking in the glossary.

Contents

What Was the Russian Revolution?

The evening of November 7, 1917, was a bitterly cold one in Petrograd. The troops who hurried through the streets of the Russian capital had their overcoats buttoned up against the winter chill. Everyone knew that something was happening. The **Bolsheviks,** a small, **left-wing** political party that had recently won the support of many of the capital's hundreds of thousands of discontented workers and soldiers, had called for revolution. Even so, theaters and restaurants were open as normal, even though the nighttime calm was sometimes broken by the rumble of distant guns.

*A dramatic **propaganda** painting shows Bolshevik soldiers and workers preparing to storm the Winter Palace in Russia's capital city. In fact, the building was not heavily defended.*

By midnight, the Winter Palace was the center of attention. It was here that the **czar,** Russia's powerful ruler, had lived when he was in his capital city. Now, the nation no longer had a czar. Instead, the palace housed representatives of the **Provisional Government,** set up eight months earlier to rule the country in the czar's place. Many of the troops guarding the palace had joined the Bolshevik revolutionaries, so only a few hundred soldiers remained behind to protect it. They were no match for the Bolsheviks' well-armed **Red Guards.** When the revolutionaries finally came, shortly after midnight, the troops guarding the palace gave in almost without a fight. Within just a few hours, the Bolsheviks had taken control of the capital city. Just months before, they had represented only a tiny minority of the country.

The year of two revolutions

The fall of the Winter Palace was the final act in an amazing drama. During 1917, Russia had experienced two separate revolutions. At the start of the year, power was still in the hands of the czar, as it had been for the past 350 years. For almost a century, though, opposition to these all-powerful rulers had been growing, as new ideas of **democracy** and progress spread across Europe. In March 1917, the Russian people, exhausted after three disastrous years of fighting against Germany and **Austria-Hungary** in World War I, had risen up and overthrown the last of their czars, Nicholas II. Russia had seemed to be on the verge of democracy at last.

In reality, though, things had gone wrong from the start. The Provisional Government, uniting all the nation's democratic forces, had struggled to maintain control in the face of mounting chaos, just as the czar had done earlier. One political party had stood outside this Provisional Government, mocking its efforts. This was the Bolshevik Party, who called instead for all-out revolution under the slogan of "Peace, Land, and Bread." As things went from bad to worse in World War I and hunger spread across the land, the Bolsheviks' simple message had won growing support. At last, on November 7, they struck. After just eight months, democracy had failed. Russia had moved from one kind of **dictatorship** to another. Now, instead of the uncontrolled czar being in power, Russia was to be ruled by the unelected leaders of the Bolshevik Party.

Czar Nicholas II in 1894 at the beginning of his reign. The last czar of Russia had little understanding of the changes that were taking place in his country. He was blamed for Russian defeats in World War I and was forced to give up his throne in March 1917.

Revolution

Revolution is the violent overthrow of a system of government and its replacement by another. Two such major upheavals in modern times were the American Revolution, which started in 1775, and the French Revolution of 1789. More recent examples include the **communist** takeover of China in 1949 and Fidel Castro's seizure of power in Cuba ten years later. The word revolution can also be used to describe other great changes in history such as the Industrial Revolution, which introduced the use of machines to produce goods that previously had been made by hand.

Russia Under the Czars

The land of the **czars** was vast. Stretching 5,000 miles (8,000 kilometers) from the German border to the Pacific Ocean, it covered one-sixth of the world's land area and spread across the two continents of Europe and Asia. Russians themselves made up less than half of its rapidly growing population, which had reached 130 million by the year 1900. Finns, Poles, Ukrainians, Armenians, Mongols, and dozens of other groups also lived in Russia. These groups spoke many different languages and dialects, practiced different religions, and were all linked only by the czar's rule.

A land of peasants

While the Industrial Revolution had brought new wealth to rival nations such as Great Britain and Germany, Russia remained mostly a land of peasants. Peasants made up four-fifths of Russia's population. Some people alive in 1917 could still remember a time when the peasants had been **serfs,** bound to serve the owner of the land on which they were born. Serfdom had finally been ended by Czar Alexander II in 1861. Although there had been great hopes for a new Russia at the time, the lives of the people had hardly changed at all. In years of bad harvests, famine and starvation were common, often taking the lives of the old, the young, and the sick.

Even so, Russia as a whole had not stood still. Under a capable minister of finance, Count Sergei Witte, the country had started to **industrialize.** The Trans-Siberian Railroad, the most ambitious engineering project of its day, had been built, making it possible to travel all the way from Moscow to the Pacific Ocean. In a half-dozen different centers, mostly in European Russia, heavy industry gained a foothold. In the 1890s, the Russian economy as a whole grew at a rate that was the highest in all of Europe.

The Russian Empire in 1900.

The Russian Empire

The plight of the poor

Although some things in Russia were improving, many fundamental problems remained. To begin with, the new wealth was not evenly spread. Even in the cities where the new industries were based, the workers who manned the factories lived in wretched poverty. A survey in 1904 revealed that those workers who had homes were living on average six to a room, while others slept on planks of wood beside their machines at the factories where they worked. The rural areas, where most of the Russian people lived, saw little benefit from the new money. If anything, the peasants were worse off, because taxes had to be raised to help pay for the new factories and railroads.

Tied together in a chain, women haul a barge along the Volga River in 1913. In many parts of Russia, rulers treated peasants as little better than animals.

The education system remained primitive. In 1897 only one in five of the population could read or write. The sheer size of the country was itself a problem, with many borders to defend. The czar's administration, which included provincial governors, police, and soldiers, was stretched too thin.

It would have taken an exceptional ruler to successfully govern this vast, underdeveloped land. Unfortunately, Nicholas II, who came to the throne at the age of 26 after his father, Alexander III, died in 1894, was not up to the job. A devoted family man, Nicholas II, or Nicholas Romanov, as he was also known, had little interest in or talent for ruling. Yet he clung to the notion that it was his duty not to share power. This stubborn attitude would eventually lead to his downfall.

Nicholas the autocrat

Despite his famous charm, Czar Nicholas II had no sympathy for reform, and thought that his duty was to pass on to his son all the royal powers he himself had inherited. On coming to the throne, he announced: *"Everyone should know that in devoting all my strength on behalf of the welfare of my people, I shall defend the principle of **autocracy** as unswervingly as my dead father."*

The Revolutionaries

The **czar's** view that the people should have no say in governing Russia was being challenged. Ever since the American and the French revolutions in the late 1700s, ideas of **democracy** and **human rights** had spread throughout Europe. People had been raising their voices and demanding greater political freedom. But such talk in Russia was still dangerous. Anyone questioning the czar's power was treated as a traitor and was in danger of being arrested. He or she could be imprisoned or **exiled** in the remote frozen wastes of Siberia in eastern Russia.

Terror and counterterror

Without any legal means of discussing their grievances, some people turned to secret plotting. One group who plotted against the czar, the Decembrists, sought only to put limits on the power of the ruler. But when five Decembrist leaders were executed in 1825 for their actions, further generations of **radicals** turned to more extreme measures. In response, the czars' ministers created a powerful secret police force to hunt down the revolutionaries, and a deadly cat-and-mouse game of terror and counterterror began. Things intensified in 1881, when a group called the People's Will succeeded in **assassinating** Alexander II, the reforming czar who had freed the **serfs.**

*Russian society as seen in a pre-1914 political cartoon. The czar and the **aristocracy** are at the top level. They are supported by the Church, the army, and the wealthy middle classes, all resting on the shoulders of the long-suffering workers and peasants.*

Those responsible for Alexander's murder were hunted down and executed, but other groups sprang up in their place. By the start of the twentieth century, they were grouped into two main factions. One, the **Social Revolutionaries,** had deep roots in the Russian countryside and sought to stir the peasants to revolt. The peasants made up the bulk of the nation's population. Some sought to achieve this goal peacefully, through **propaganda** and persuasion, but there was also a radical, armed section of the movement dedicated to terror and political assassination. Over the next twenty years, the list of their victims lengthened. It included one prime minister and three other senior ministers, an uncle of a czar, the governor general of Finland, and several high-ranking police officials. One casualty was V. K. Plehve, who was a much-feared minister of the interior. He had been the czar's right-hand man and was the radicals' fiercest opponent.

Karl Marx

Karl Marx (1818–1883) was a German philosopher who spent much of his life in exile. He believed that the struggle between different classes of society was the driving force behind history, and that ultimately power would end up in the hands of the working class because they were responsible for creating the wealth of nations. His ideas were hugely influential and helped to inspire **communism,** the political movement dedicated to creating a more equal society in which private property is abolished.

Bolsheviks and Mensheviks

The other main wing of the revolutionary movement was made up by the **Social Democrats,** who drew their strength from the cities. They shared the views of the German political philosopher Karl Marx, who believed that the tide of history must inevitably put power in the hands of the industrial **working class.** In 1903, however, the movement split into two rival wings that were divided over the best way to bring about a working-class revolution. One group thought that the only way to achieve its goal was through a tightly disciplined party carrying out the decisions of a small, dedicated leadership group. The other group wanted a more **democratic** approach, opening up the party to all who wished to join and accepting the will of the majority in decision making. Because political activity was banned in Russia, the group leaders met in Brussels, Belgium. There, the dispute grew. The first group carried the majority vote at the conference and from that time on bore the name of **Bolsheviks,** meaning "the majority." Their opponents became known as the **Mensheviks,** or "minority." Ironically, that vote was an exceptional one, because for most of the time up to the 1917 revolution the Mensheviks had greater popular support.

Other groups also refused to accept the existing political situation in Russia. Anarchists wanted to bring down Russia's leaders by any means necessary, while liberals sought parliamentary democracy along **Western** European lines. This liberal group became known as the Constitutional Democrats, or **Cadets** for short. They had given up violence in favor of peaceful change, and they too were to play an important part in the 1917 revolution.

The German political philosopher Karl Marx, coauthor of The **Communist** *Manifesto, was a guiding light for both the Bolshevik and Menshevik wings of the Social Democratic Party.*

9

Lenin

The man who did more than any other to transform the old Russia was born Vladimir Ulyanov in the city of Simbirsk on the Volga River in 1870. He was 30 years old when he adopted the name Lenin, borrowed from the Lena River in Siberia. The future revolutionary was the son of upper-middle-class parents. His father had the important job of school inspector, so ordinary people had to address him as "Your Excellency." As a boy, Vladimir enjoyed a carefree childhood on the family estate until 1887, when an event happened that changed his life. His elder brother Alexander, a student who had become involved in **radical** politics, was arrested for his part in a plot to kill **Czar** Alexander III. He had made the bomb that was to be used to blow up the ruler and was subsequently hanged, along with four of his fellow plotters.

This oil painting shows the young Lenin comforting his mother as she grieves for her eldest son, who was executed in 1887 for his part in a plot to kill the czar.

Deeply shocked, Lenin himself took up where his brother had left off. He was expelled from the University of Kazan for political activities, but was eventually allowed to return in 1891 to complete his training as a lawyer. He then moved to Russia's capital, St. Petersburg—later to be renamed Petrograd—where he soon came to the attention of the secret police. Arrested for revolutionary activities, he spent a year in prison and was then **exiled** to Siberia for three more years. By the time he returned to St. Petersburg in 1900, Lenin was a confirmed **Marxist.** He was convinced that revolution would come from the industrial **working class.** He had also developed the view that the revolution should be led by a small group of dedicated revolutionaries. He would later champion this idea when he became leader of the **Bolsheviks.**

Life in exile

Lenin spent the next seventeen years up to the revolution in exile in Western Europe, keeping out of reach of the czar's police. There he wrote pamphlets, attended conferences of Russian opposition parties, and edited newspapers that were smuggled into Russia. Although he devoted his life to the cause of the workers and peasants, he had little contact with them as people and could be ruthless in his attitude toward them. In 1891, he argued against providing food

aid to starving peasants on the grounds that hunger was likely to make them more radical. Having taken up the cause of revolution, he gave his entire life to it. When the chance came in 1917, his extraordinary single-mindedness was to play a decisive part in the Bolshevik victory.

As Lenin was starting his long exile, other leading players were also taking up the revolutionary cause. In the southern region of Russia called Georgia, Joseph Djugashvili, the son of a shoemaker, gave up training to become a priest. He then turned to the life of a bandit, robbing banks to raise money for **left-wing** causes. He would later rise to fame as Lenin's eventual successor, the **dictator** Joseph Stalin. Another revolutionary who changed his name was Lev Davidovitch Bronstein. He became known as Leon Trotsky. For a long while Trotsky was a **Menshevik,** but he later worked closely with Lenin to establish the Bolshevik state. After Lenin's death, Trotsky and Stalin became bitter rivals in the race to succeed Lenin.

Unlike the political prisoners pictured here, Lenin was not imprisoned or forced to do hard labor during his three-year exile in Siberia. In fact, he was able to carry on with his revolutionary writings.

Lenin the man

In *Ten Days that Shook the World*, the American journalist John Reed described the impression that Bolshevik leader Lenin made upon him in 1917: *"A short, stocky figure with a big head set down on his shoulders, bald and bulging. Little eyes, a snubbish nose, wide, generous mouth and heavy chin; clean-shaven now but beginning to bristle with the well-known beard. Dressed in shabby clothes, his trousers much too long for him. Unimpressive, to be the idol of a mob, loved and worshiped as perhaps few leaders in history have been."*

The Gathering Storm

In 1901, after ten years of rapid expansion, the Russian economy hit a rocky road. In line with a general European slowdown, annual economic growth rates in Russia fell drastically. At the same time, a string of bad harvests brought hunger in their wake.

In rural regions, more people began to express their discontent. Even after the abolition of **serfdom,** it was difficult for peasants to own land. All land that was not part of the **noblemen's** estates was the property of the village **commune,** which divided the land into strips called plots and assigned them to individual families. Most households could not make a living from the plot alone, so the sons had to spend part of each year either working on noblemen's estates or in the cities, laboring in factories. By the 1900s, there were about nine million of these traveling workers, most of them young and restless.

Unemployed workers eat a meal in St. Petersburg before World War I.

Meanwhile, the workers in the cities were also unhappy. Wages were low and working conditions were bad. **Trade unions** were banned, so there was no way for working people to make their feelings known except to go on **strike,** which they often did.

In response, from 1900 onward the police authorities themselves secretly helped to set up some workers' associations. They hoped to channel the workers' anger into organizations that remained loyal to the **czar.** However, the strategy backfired. So many people flocked to join these associations that the government quickly grew nervous and stopped lending its support.

Life in the cities

Life for workers in the cities could be grim. One factory employee described conditions in Moscow in 1900: *"I lived near the factory, in a large, smelly house inhabited by various poor people. About fifteen of us rented one apartment. I was in a dark, windowless corner room. It was dirty and stuffy, full of bedbugs and fleas. There was just room for two wooden beds. I shared mine with one other man. The rooms stank of the mud from the streets, which was made up of dirt, rubbish and sewage."*

Even the upper middle classes were restless for change. Doctors, lawyers, and businessmen were often highly educated. They bitterly resented the fact that, because all political power remained in the hands of the czar, they had no say in the running of the country. Some had become involved in the *zemstvos,* which were local councils first set up under the reforming Czar Alexander II in 1864 to provide some regional welfare services such as schools and hospitals. The zemstvo activists mostly shared a taste for social reform with a belief in **Western** parliamentary **democracy.**

Under the gaze of an Orthodox priest, coffins of Russian soldiers killed in the Russo-Japanese War of 1904–1905 are loaded onto wagons for transport to burial grounds.

The Russo-Japanese war

In 1904 the growing rumble of unrest led the czar's ministers to make a fatal error. In East Asia, a dispute with Japan over trading rights in Korea and northern China was escalating. Rather than settle the problem through **diplomacy,** the government decided to run the risk of entering what one minister called "a short, victorious war" in the hope of uniting the country behind the czar. But when the Japanese attacked in 1904, Russia's armed forces were taken by surprise. Russia suffered a number of humiliating defeats. The defeats were also highly unexpected because the Russian government had badly underestimated the fighting ability of their Japanese enemy.

Far from solidifying support for the czar, the string of military disasters brought the nation's simmering discontent to the boiling point. The war disrupted transportation, increased government spending, and brought further food shortages. Strikes and demonstrations broke out in many parts of the country, and there was a series of terrorist **assassinations.** Defeat showed that the government was not just **dictatorial** but also inefficient. The angry public was ready for revolt.

Bloody Sunday

The trigger for revolt came in January 1905 with a **strike** at St. Petersburg's giant Putilov ironworks. Workers elsewhere in the city laid down their tools in sympathy, and soon much of the city's industry was at a standstill. Then, one of the unions recently set up with secret police support came to the forefront. Its leader was a priest, Father Georgi Gapon. Though fervently loyal to **Czar** Nicholas II, he decided to lead a demonstration to the Winter Palace to present the people's complaints to the ruler. Surely, he thought, Nicholas would hear their complaints and take steps to correct them.

On Sunday, January 22, Gapon led the crowd of about 150,000 toward the Winter Palace, singing hymns and carrying religious images. The demonstrators were unarmed and included many women and children. Knowing the brutal reputation of the czar's guards, however, some people expected trouble. All too soon their fears were realized. When the marchers reached the palace, they were met by a line of soldiers who fired two warning shots into the air and then fired directly into the crowd, killing 40 people. The crowd scattered. Throughout the day there were further bloody clashes with troops, and in all, about 200 people died.

As news of the "Bloody Sunday" massacre spread across Russia, the effect on people's attitudes was dramatic. Until then, most people had believed that the czar—the Father of the Nation—was on their side, even if his government was cruel and incompetent. Now that faith was largely gone. Father Gapon himself wrote bitterly, "We no longer have a czar. Today a river of blood divides him from the Russian people."

The chaos spreads

Over the following months, as the war with Japan went from bad to worse, violence spread across the land. In Russia's rural areas, there was a wave of attacks on **noblemen's** homes, and nearly 3,000 houses were burned down. This was almost one-sixth of the total number of houses across the nation. In the cities, crime rates soared and a wave of strikes paralyzed industry and the railroads, making it impossible to bring the troops back from the battlefront in East Asia. Members of Russia's minority groups saw the widespread breakdown of law and order as an opportunity to reach for freedom. The chaos continued to spread. In Poland, there was fighting in the streets. In Finland, the Russian governor general was **assassinated,** and for a time, parts of the Georgia region broke away entirely from government control.

Disgruntled by defeat, many military units **mutinied.** The crew of one battleship, the *Potemkin,* seized control of the vessel and sailed it across the Black Sea to Romania. The wave of terrorist assassinations increased. One of the victims was the czar's uncle, Grand Duke Sergei. Seeking people to blame

for the troubles, **right-wing** gangs launched attacks on Jewish communities, killing an estimated 3,000 people.

Rise of the soviets

In Moscow and St. Petersburg, the troubles came to a head in September and October with a general strike that brought industry to a standstill. To bring some sort of order to the chaos, the workers set up **soviets**—a Russian word meaning "councils"—to

keep basic services functioning. Soon these were virtually running the cities. Sensing revolution in the air, some political **exiles** slipped back into Russia. Trotsky became a leader of the St. Petersburg soviet, ending up as its chairman, but Lenin arrived late and played little part in the uprising.

In fact, the 1905 uprising had taken the revolutionaries by surprise as much as it had the government. Springing up in many different places for many different causes, it was formless and uncontrolled. For a time, at least, Russia seemed to be falling apart.

*Taken in October 1905, this photo shows workers parading through St. Petersburg carrying banners calling for **democratic** reforms and an end to one-man rule by the czar.*

The October Manifesto

Russia was saved from total collapse in 1905 largely because the various uprisings were uncontrolled. Together, they might have been unstoppable, but separately each one could be put down by the **czar's** forces.

A vital first step toward restoring order was ending the war with Japan. As it turned out, Count Sergei Witte was able to make peace with Japan on surprisingly favorable terms at the Treaty of Portsmouth, which was signed in September. Even so, the nation remained in chaos, and the general **strike** that had been called in the cities threatened to make it ungovernable and uncontrollable. In October, Witte presented the czar with a stark choice—either he would have to appoint a military **dictator** to restore order by force or make concessions to his opponents, who were demanding **democratic** reform. Initially Nicholas favored the first idea, but his choice of dictator, Grand Duke Nikolai Nikolaevich, threatened to shoot himself if Nicholas refused to bow to public opinion. The czar unwillingly agreed to sign the document that Witte had prepared.

This anti-czarist **propaganda** *image shows the October Manifesto imprinted with a bloody hand. The hand was meant to represent the czar not allowing a democratic government.*

This document, which became known as the "October Manifesto," announced that for the first time in its history Russia would have an elected parliament, called the **Duma.** Political parties and **trade unions** were legalized, **censorship** was to be lifted, and some **political prisoners** were set free.

Life returns to normal

The manifesto was a limited move in the direction of reform, because the parliament would only be able to advise the czar, not make laws. It was enough, however, to split the opposition to the czar. The liberals at once withdrew their support for the general strike, which quickly crumbled. With peace and the ending of the rail strike, troops began to return from

The world turned upside down

In Boris Pasternak's novel *Doctor Zhivago*, a train conductor's widow gives her son news of the October Manifesto, expressing the hopes it aroused among ordinary people for better times ahead: *"Think of it! The czar has signed a manifesto and everything's to be turned upside down! Everybody's to be treated right, the peasants are to have land, and we're all going to be equal with the* **gentry!***"*

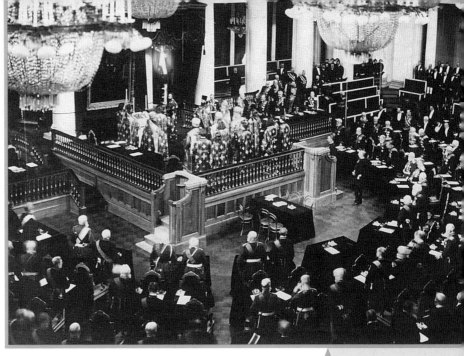

battlefields in East Asia and were quickly used to restore order. The St. Petersburg **soviet** was broken up, as were those in other cities. In Moscow, this led to street fighting that claimed more than 1,000 lives. The violence in the countryside proved even more difficult to stop. It surged up again in 1906 and was only stopped with much brutality. As many as 15,000 people are thought to have been executed.

The October Manifesto had raised great hopes, but in the end the hopes were quickly crushed. Censorship was reintroduced and political prisoners were arrested again. Some revolutionaries, like Lenin, once again fled the country. Trotsky was seized when the St. Petersburg soviet was closed down, and he was **exiled** to Siberia.

Russia's first Duma

The parliamentary democracy promised in the manifesto also fell short of expectations. With order restored in 1906, the czar felt sure enough of his position to issue the "Fundamental Laws." These reasserted his own unrestricted authority. The laws stated bluntly that "the All-Russian Emperor possesses the supreme **autocratic** power; not only fear and conscience, but God himself, command obedience to his authority." In keeping with this view, Nicholas treated the Duma with barely hidden contempt. When the first Duma proved too **radical** for his liking, he simply dissolved it. A second Duma suffered a similar fate. To make the Duma more compliant, he ordered a change to the electoral rules. When the third Duma was called in 1907, two-thirds of its delegates were elected by the richest people in Russia.

Even so, order had been restored, and a strife-weary population mostly seemed happy to get back to normal life. On the surface little had changed, but in reality the czar's position had been seriously weakened. He was never to exercise the same unchallenged authority again.

The Coming of World War I

By agreeing to set up the **Duma,** the **czar** had managed to split the groups opposed to his rule. Those who wanted parliamentary **democracy** similar to that in **Western** European countries—mostly the middle classes—were generally happy for the time being to give the new body a chance. Workers and peasants were still unhappy, but they were not strong enough on their own to bring the system down. It seemed that czarist Russia had survived.

Stolypin's strong measures

To make his position stronger, Nicholas II turned to an able administrator, Peter Stolypin. The son of landowning **aristocrats,** Stolypin believed in the need for strong measures to help save the nation. First, he cracked down on the **left-wing** parties by closing **trade unions** and left-wing newspapers. Then, he introduced **radical** reforms of his own in the countryside. Peasants could, for the first time, leave the village **communes** and own their own land. The idea was that the most ambitious peasants would develop into a class of independent small landholders who would respect property rights and be loyal to the czar.

Stolypin's reforms attracted bitter hostility, both from traditionalist peasants, who feared the loss of commune lands, and from aristocratic landowners, who saw them as a threat to their own position. Even so, the changes were effective, at least in parts of the nation. Agricultural productivity improved dramatically, and the production of grain crops also increased between 1908 and 1912. At the same time, Count Sergei Witte had negotiated a huge loan from Western European bankers that got Russian industry moving again. The country's yearly rate of growth increased drastically between 1907 and 1914, compared to what it was from 1900 to 1905. Between 1900 and 1914, coal production more than doubled, and steel production grew by more than 50 percent.

Peter Stolypin, Russia's prime minister from 1906, poses with his wife. Stolypin was assassinated at the opera house in Kiev in 1911.

The death of Stolypin

Politically, however, there was less progress. With the change Nicholas made to the electoral laws, the Duma became the mouthpiece of wealthy landowners. Without any legal means of making their voices heard, the radicals turned again to violence. Even in 1908, a relatively quiet year, some 1,800 officials were killed in political attacks across Russia. Eventually Stolypin himself fell victim. In 1911, he was shot dead while attending an opera in the city of Kiev.

Without his leadership, the czar's government again became directionless. Some ministers tried to boost support for the ruler by stirring up hostility against Russia's Jewish people, who traditionally had been targets for **right-wing** hatred. When that proved insufficient, nationalist opinion looked for foreign enemies instead. Tensions in the Balkan region just beyond Russia's southwestern border grew worse in 1914 with the **assassination** of Archduke Franz Ferdinand, the heir to the **Austro-Hungarian** throne. The army and much of the Duma urged the czar to declare war on Austria-Hungary, Russia's rival for influence in the region. Briefly Nicholas held back as other advisers pointed out that Russia's last two military campaigns, in the **Crimean** and Russo-Japanese wars, had both been disastrous for the monarchy. One had stirred up the agitation that led to the **emancipation** of the **serfs,** the other to the 1905 uprising and the October Manifesto. But in the end the voices for war were loudest. On July 30, 1914, the czar ordered a general **mobilization** of the troops. Within a week, Russia was at war not just with Austria-Hungary but with Germany as well. World War I had begun.

Taken early in World War I, this photograph shows Russian officers kneeling before Nicholas II, who is on horseback. The czar holds an icon, or a sacred painting, used to bless the soldiers.

The Shadow of Rasputin

For the first few weeks after the declaration of war, it seemed that the **czar's** gamble might pay off. The country rallied behind him for the first time in his reign. On the **Austro-Hungarian** front, the fighting went well, too. Russian forces under General Alexei Brusilov captured much of the province of Galicia. A spirit of **patriotism** swept across the nation, and St. Petersburg was even renamed Petrograd to sound more Russian. Russia was only prepared for a short war, but when German forces farther north won two crucial victories at Tannenburg and the Masurian Lakes, it became obvious that there was to be no quick victory.

Unrest in the ranks

From that time on, the war went from bad to worse. While Russia's enemies managed to feed, equip, and move their armies as needed, the Russian administration cracked under the strain. Soon, attacks were being called off because the Russian army's big guns, called artillery, had no shells. The number

Russian soldiers taken as prisoners during the early years of World War I. Russia's involvement in this war had disastrous consequences for the czar.

of Russian soldiers killed quickly rose into the millions as incompetent commanders sent waves of soldiers fighting on foot to attack positions defended by soldiers with machine guns. A mood of despair spread among the underfed, poorly clothed, and ill-armed troops. Some of the soldiers started to see their own officers, who were mostly landowners and from the class they had come to hate, as more their enemies than the Germans or Austrians.

Things were not much better away from the battlefields. The need to divert trains to carry supplies to the war front clogged up the nation's transportation system. As a result, deliveries of food and other essential goods to cities were held up. Soon, lining up for these goods was a regular part of daily life. In the face of repeated military defeats and growing shortages, the mood of patriotism soon faded and was replaced by anger and bitterness.

Despair on the front line

A report from a Russian general shows how bad things were for ordinary soldiers fighting on the front line as early as 1915: "*In recent battles, one-third of the men have had no rifles. The poor devils had to wait patiently until their comrades fell before their eyes, and they could pick up their weapons. The army is drowning in its own blood.*"

A hated queen

By August 1915, things were going so badly that the czar decided to take personal command of the army. It was an unwise decision. It meant that the czar had to take personal responsibility for the Russian army losing battles in the war. But it also left the rest of the country in the hands of his wife, Czarina Alexandra. German by birth, she was suspected unfairly of sympathizing with the enemy. She was, however, completely opposed to **democracy.** She was constantly encouraging her husband to be the **autocrat** that she was convinced Russia needed.

She was hated worst of all, though, for being influenced by the sinister Grigori Rasputin. Though only a peasant, Rasputin had a reputation as a holy man, but he was actually greedy and immoral. Nevertheless, he appeared to have real gifts as a healer. He was able to win the admiration of the royal family through his ability to relieve their son's hemophilia, a rare blood disorder that made the boy liable to uncontrolled internal bleeding after even minor bumps and scrapes. The czarina in particular came to believe that Rasputin had been sent by God

A cartoon from 1916 shows Rasputin as a sinister, looming presence, holding the czar and czarina as puppets on his knees.

to save the czar and Russia. As his influence on policy and government appointments grew, support for the monarchy dissolved. Finally, a group of the czar's supporters took the law into their own hands and murdered Rasputin in December 1916. By then, though, the damage had been done. The last remainders of respect for the czar's rule were gone. Tired of the war and disillusioned, Russia was ripe for revolution.

Rasputin's sinister powers

Prince Feliks Yusupov—one of the czar's supporters who eventually killed Rasputin—describes his first encounter with the supposed holy man: "*His hypnotic power was immense. I felt it subduing me and diffusing warmth throughout the whole of my being. I grew numb; my body seemed paralyzed. I tried to speak, but my tongue would not obey me, and I seemed to be falling asleep, as if under the influence of a strong drug. Yet Rasputin's eyes shone before me like a kind of phosphorescent light.*"

1917: The First Revolution

When the uprising that brought down the **czar** finally came, it took everyone by surprise. Even agitators who had spent their lives trying to bring it about were unprepared. Just a month before, Lenin had declared, "We older men perhaps will not live to see the coming revolution."

Russian soldiers opposing the czar pose in Petrograd at the start of the revolution. The czar was forced to step down in March 1917.

With most of the revolutionaries in prison or in **exile,** the revolution was created in the streets. The revolution began on March 8, 1917, with a demonstration of women fed up with waiting in line for bread. They rallied factory workers to their cause, and the next day **striking** workers started attacking public buildings and police stations. Troops were called out to restore order, and there were some shootings, though most of the soldiers supported the demonstrators rather than their own commanding officers. **Mutiny** spread through where the soldiers lived, and soon thousands of armed soldiers had joined the crowds in the streets. Left undefended, most of the czar's ministers and supporters went into hiding or fled.

Two power centers

After the uprising, the old government quite simply collapsed. Out of the chaos, two separate power centers emerged, both housed at first in different wings of Petrograd's Tauride Palace. One was the **Provisional Government,** set up by party leaders in the **Duma.** It was called provisional because it was seen at the time as a temporary arrangement until a proper government could be established. The other was the Petrograd **Soviet** of Workers' and Soldiers' **Deputies,** a revival of the organization set up in 1905.

With chaos and crime spreading in the streets, the first job was to restore order. The Provisional Government sought to do so in the name of parliamentary **democracy,** and the Soviet agreed to lend its support as long as its own demands were met. These demands included an end to **censorship,** the release of all **political prisoners,** and the creation of people's **militias** to replace the old czarist police. Both bodies supported free elections for a **Constituent Assembly,** to be chosen by all the people.

The czar steps down

That left the question of what to do with the czar. On hearing of the trouble in Petrograd, he had ordered troops to the capital city to attack the demonstrators only to find that the troops refused to obey him. Without the support of the troops, he was powerless. There were still some **right-wing** leaders in the Duma who wanted him to still rule like a king. His position would have been like that of the British monarch. While he still would have been the head of state, he would have had no political power. But the idea was quickly dropped. Others thought he should abdicate, or give up the crown, in favor of his son. Nicholas himself ruled out that idea, knowing that his son was too sickly to be czar. Representatives from the Duma then approached Nicholas's brother, the Grand Duke Michael, and asked him to take over. When he refused the offer on March 16, one thousand years of rule by monarchy came abruptly to an end.

The Provisional Government was now in control, but it inherited all the problems that had brought down the czar, plus one more. Power was divided between the Assembly and the Soviet bodies. Until the new Constituent Assembly could be called—the elections were eventually arranged for November—it could not claim to be democratically elected. The Soviet, in contrast, had huge popular support from the army and the factories, but no part in government. In the joyful March days, when all the talk was of the two bodies sharing "dual power," it seemed that contradictions could be overcome if everyone worked together. In fact, though, it was only to be a matter of weeks before strains began to show.

The Soviet of Workers' and Soldiers' Deputies meets in Petrograd's Tauride Palace in April 1917. The soviets were political organizations made up of workers, soldiers, and sailors who were more **radical** than the members of the Provisional Government.

The czar's legacy

Alexander Kerensky, who served in the Provisional Government first as minister of justice and then as prime minister, summed up its situation on taking power: "[The Government] *inherited nothing from the czar but a terrible war, an acute food shortage, a paralyzed transportation system, an empty treasury, and a population in a state of furious discontent . . .*"

The Democratic Experiment

Although people could see that difficulties were ahead, most of Russia greeted the **czar's** downfall with joy. In a spirit of cooperation, almost all the political parties agreed to put their differences temporarily aside to work together for **democracy.** The **Provisional Government** was dominated by middle-class liberals of the Constitutional Democratic party, known as the **Cadets,** but it could count on the support of the two main **left-wing** parties, the **Mensheviks** and the **Social Revolutionaries.**

Soon, the Provisional Government set about putting through the reforms that so many people had sought for so long. **Censorship** was abolished, and there was to be absolute freedom of speech. **Trade unions** and **strikes** were legalized. All the different groups of people within the Russian empire were to have equal rights, and outlying regions such as Finland and Poland, which were then both part of Russia, were to have a say in running their own affairs. All **political prisoners** were freed, and the death sentence was abolished.

Problems that would not go away

The big problems that had confronted the czar's government, however, were not so easy to deal with. Conditions in the cities continued to get worse as food shortages increased. By 1917, there were two million soldiers who had deserted the army. They joined the ranks of the unemployed and lived by committing street crimes. As for the factory workers, their expectations had been raised by the overthrow of the czar, and they increasingly demanded a say in running industry.

In the country's rural areas, the peasants were also impatient for change. The Provisional Government had postponed land reform until the **Constituent Assembly** could be called. Those living in village **communes** grew tired of waiting, though, and increasingly took the law into their own hands, seizing land from its private owners. Mobs started burning the owners' houses again, as they had in 1905.

Worst of all, World War I refused to go away. The people of the country were tired of the war, and the soldiers wanted above all to get back home. But the Provisional Government felt that it had a duty to the nation not to give in. Besides, its ministers were under pressure from Russia's **allies,** Great Britain and France, to keep on fighting.

A Bolshevik-era painting shows Lenin arriving from exile, greeting a crowd at Petrograd's Finland Station on April 3, 1917. The Germans had let him pass through their territory in the hope that he would weaken the Russian war effort.

Lenin returns from exile

In addition to its other problems, the Provisional Government faced opposition from one significant party on the left: the **Bolsheviks.** In April their leader, Lenin, arrived back from **exile** to a hero's welcome at Petrograd's Finland Station. He had traveled by arrangement with Russia's German enemies, who, hoping that he would stir up trouble, had transported him from his home in Switzerland through Germany in a special sealed train. Within days of his arrival, he announced his program. It included total opposition to the Provisional Government, an immediate end to the war, the arming of the workers, and the passing of all power to the **soviets.** At first, even his own Bolshevik supporters were shocked. Russia had just experienced one revolution, and now Lenin was calling for another. Critics called his views the ravings of a madman, but upcoming events were to prove them wrong.

Discontent in the cities

Fully stretched by the war effort, the Provisional Government could do little to improve life for people who lived in cities on the home front. Journalist John Reed described life in Petrograd in 1917: "*At night the street lights were few; in private houses the electricity was turned off from six o'clock until midnight. Robberies and house-breaking increased. In apartments men took turns at all night guard duty, armed with loaded rifles . . . Food was becoming scarce. The daily allowance of bread fell. There were times when no bread at all was available. For milk, bread, sugar, and tobacco one had to [wait in line] for long hours in the cold rain.*

Of course, life for the rich went on much the same. The theaters were going every night, including Sundays."

The Bolshevik Takeover

Under pressure to reunite the nation, the **Provisional Government** made a bad mistake. In July 1917, it ordered a military advance in Galicia, an area in the northeast of **Austria-Hungary.** This advance was quickly overwhelmed by a German counterattack, which caused the Russian army to retreat. They suffered more than 200,000 casualties.

Russia and Europe in 1914–1917.

Area lost under Treaty of Brest-Litovsk
★ Battles
〜 Eastern Front

FINLAND
Petrograd
Baltic Sea
Moscow
RUSSIAN EMPIRE
Tannenberg ★ Masurian Lakes
GERMAN EMPIRE
Brest-Litovsk
Kiev
Galicia   UKRAINE
AUSTRO-HUNGARIAN EMPIRE
ROMANIA
BULGARIA
Black Sea
GEORGIA
Caspian Sea
OTTOMAN EMPIRE

0   miles   500
0   km   500

The "July days"

The government's move was deeply unpopular, and by mid–July armed mobs filled the streets of Petrograd, demanding that the government step down. The **Bolsheviks** had encouraged people to start the riots. The "July days," as the riots became known, were a rehearsal for the uprising that finally brought down the Provisional Government in November, but now they had come too soon. Without leaders to direct them, the riots fell apart and the people went home.

In the wake of the riots, the **socialist** Alexander Kerensky took over as the Provisional Government's leader and at once launched an assault on the Bolsheviks, whom he blamed for the unrest. Lenin, he claimed, was a German spy, trying to stir up trouble at a time when the Russian army was fighting for its life. For a time, public opinion supported him. The Bolsheviks' headquarters was shut down by police, several of their leaders were arrested, and Lenin himself had to escape in disguise to Finland.

The mood across Russia was by now feverish. Kerensky had the job of trying to hold together a country that was increasingly divided. The spirit of cooperation that had marked the downfall of the **czar** was largely gone.

The Kornilov affair

To restore order, Kerensky appointed a new commander of the army, Lavr Kornilov, and for a time toyed with the idea of summoning him to Petrograd to put down the Bolsheviks once and for all. But fearing that the general intended to seize power for himself, Kerensky gave orders instead for his dismissal. Kornilov refused to step down. Instead, he decided to advance on Petrograd without Kerensky's permission.

Fearing a **right-wing** takeover, Kerensky now looked to the **left-wing** for support. He gave orders that workers should be armed. Kornilov, meanwhile, had found that his own troops were unwilling to obey him. His last hopes of advancing on the capital faded when **striking** railroad workers prevented him from transporting his forces on trains to the city.

Pro-democracy demonstrators gather in Petrograd for a mass rally in 1917.

The Kornilov affair finished off Kerensky's chances of keeping the current government going. Without army support, he had no troops of his own to set against the Bolshevik **Red Guard,** who had seized most of the rifles and machine guns handed out to workers in order to fight off Kornilov. Fearing that the revolution was in danger from the generals, workers now flocked to join the Bolsheviks, whose slogans of "Peace, Land, and Bread" and "All Power to the **Soviets**" increasingly matched with the popular mood.

Now Lenin saw his chance. Against the wishes of most Bolsheviks, he argued that the party must strike at once, saying, "History will not forgive us if we do not take power now." Lenin's appeals became more and more popular, and his wishes were granted. Trotsky organized a military uprising. On November 6, 1917, Red Guards occupied key points across the city of Petrograd, and on the following day, with the fall of the Winter Palace, the Provisional Government itself fell into the hands of the Bolsheviks. Kerensky fled the city. Stunned, the people of Russia learned that there had been another revolution. The Bolsheviks were now in charge of Russia.

Proclaiming the revolution

On the day the Bolsheviks launched their bid for power, Lenin released this declaration:
"TO THE CITIZENS OF RUSSIA!
The Provisional Government has been deposed . . .

*The cause for which the people have been struggling—the immediate offer of a **democratic** peace, the abolition of landlord property rights over the land, worker control over production, the creation of a Soviet Government—this cause has been achieved.*

Long live the revolution of Workers, Soldiers, and Peasants!"

Building Socialism

Even the **Bolsheviks** themselves were surprised at how easily they had seized power, and they quickly took steps to make sure they would keep it. To the surprise of many of his own followers, Lenin refused to cooperate with the **Mensheviks** and most of the other **socialist** parties. Instead, he set up a Council of People's **Commissars,** which was controlled by Bolsheviks. Meanwhile, going back on earlier promises of freedom of speech, he outlawed the **Cadets**—the main **right-wing** opposition party—and closed down newspapers supporting other political groups.

Even Lenin, however, could not stop the **Constituent Assembly** from meeting. For half a century, the idea of a freely elected parliament had been the hope of those seeking a more **democratic** Russia, and the elections had been called for shortly after the Bolsheviks seized power. When the results came in, however, they were not at all to Lenin's liking. The Bolshevik Party had won only one-quarter of the vote, giving it 170 seats out of a total of 707. The **Social Revolutionary** Party, on the other hand, had won 370 seats, thanks to its backing among the peasants.

Overruling democracy

Lenin, however, had no intention of giving up power. Instead, he chose to overrule democracy. He sent troops to prevent the Constituent Assembly from meeting. His partner in power, Trotsky, instructed the delegates to go home, telling them, "Your role is finished, and you may go where you belong—on the garbage heap of history." Soldiers opened fire on demonstrators protesting the Assembly's closing, killing at least ten people.

Meanwhile, Lenin set about building socialism by **decree.** With extraordinary speed, the Council of People's Commissars pushed through a mind-boggling number of revolutionary measures aimed at transforming the basis of Russian society. Private ownership of land was abolished, and the peasant **communes** were encouraged to seize landowners' property. Banks and much of industry was **nationalized.** All **aristocratic** titles were done away with. From that time on, every person was to be known simply as "citizen" or "comrade."

The Bolsheviks wanted to educate workers, as this literacy campaign poster shows. The book's text in the poster compares books to public speakers.

The old criminal courts were replaced by revolutionary tribunals in which anyone could appear as a lawyer. Men and women were declared equal under the law, and divorce between married couples was to be made easy. The **stock market** ceased to exist. All of Russia's existing debts to foreign nations and bankers were cancelled, and private inheritance of goods and property was banned. The Orthodox Church lost its privileged position and was expected to pay the state rent for its churches, and religious education was banned in schools. In the rush to get rid of the past, the old Russian calendar, which ran thirteen days behind the **Western** one, was replaced. The nation's capital city was also changed. Moscow, not Petrograd, was now the capital.

The price of peace

The main reason for the move to Moscow was the looming presence of enemy troops, for Bolshevik power still faced another threat that could not be dealt with as easily as the Constituent Assembly. The German army was now within striking distance of Petrograd itself. Despite protests from his own supporters, Lenin decided that the survival of the revolution required peace at any price. When terms were agreed in the **Treaty** of Brest-Litovsk, signed in March 1918, they were disastrous for Russia. The nation lost huge amounts of land in the Baltic region, Poland, the Ukraine, and Georgia. In all, the losses cost Russia one-third of its population, more than a quarter of its agricultural land, a third of its industry, and nine-tenths of its coal mines. It was a heavy price to pay for the survival of the revolution.

Lenin, wearing a long, dark coat, is pictured here with other Bolshevik officials in Moscow's Red Square. To escape the German armies, the Bolshevik government was moved from Petrograd to Moscow in March of 1918.

Peace at any price

Early in 1918, Lenin explained to the Petrograd **soviet** why he thought it necessary to accept the harsh German terms for making peace: *"To carry on a revolutionary war we need an army, and we do not have one. It is a question of signing terms now, or of signing the death of the Soviet government three weeks later."*

The Fate of the Romanovs

*A 1919 **propaganda** poster shows workers raising blades to slay a monster representing the power and wealth of the privileged classes. The monster has wrapped itself around the factories where wealth is created.*

Meanwhile, the **Bolsheviks'** seizure of power had not gone unchallenged inside Russia. Immediately after the November **coup,** the deposed leader of the **Provisional Government,** Alexander Kerensky, had tried to rally support in the army. Only a few troops backed him, however, and they were defeated by Bolshevik forces known as the **Red Guards** outside Petrograd. Kerensky himself escaped into **exile.** Then, when the Bolsheviks' intention to rule alone became known, railroad workers and civil servants went on **strike** against the new government. There were even splits in the Bolshevik Party itself. At one point, four of its leading members resigned in protest at Lenin's tactics, only to return to the party shortly afterward.

Lenin responded stubbornly to all these challenges. The strikes were declared illegal, and the workers gradually drifted back to their jobs. A secret police organization, the **Cheka,** was set up to spy on political opponents. It would soon become even more feared than the secret police that had operated under the **czars.** Unrest in the cities was stamped out by armed Red Guards, and in Moscow there was a week of street fighting that ended in a victory for the Bolsheviks.

The opposition gathers strength

Thwarted in the main cities, the Bolsheviks' opponents now started forming groups in outlying parts of the country. General Kornilov, along with several leading figures from the old Provisional Government, made his way to the Don region of southern Russia to join **Cossack** rebels there. Meanwhile, a legion of Czech soldiers who had fought on the Russian side in the war now became involved in conflicts with Red Guards and took up arms against the Bolsheviks. Intent on fighting their way across Russia to the Pacific port of Vladivostok, they took control of the Trans-Siberian Railroad, cutting the government in Petrograd off from the East-Asian provinces.

The Czechs' triumphal progress eastward was to have an unforeseen consequence that was to prove fatal for the former royal family. After the February revolution, Nicholas II and the rest of the Romanov family had at first lived at their estate outside Petrograd, taking no part in politics and enjoying the quiet family life for which they had always been best suited. As the revolutionary temperature rose, however, the Provisional Government had transferred the czar and his family for their own safety to Tobolsk, a rural town in Siberia.

In the spring of 1918, the new Bolshevik administration ordered the family to be moved again, this time to the town of Ekaterinburg near the Ural Mountains. There, on the night of July 17, 1918, with the Czech legion approaching, the entire family was murdered, along with their doctor, their remaining servant, and even their pet spaniel. At the time, the Bolshevik government blamed the killing on the local **soviet,** some of whom were subsequently put on trial. Now, however, it is known that the order had come from Moscow, and probably from Lenin himself. He was known to be concerned that **counterrevolutionaries** might use the ex-czar as a figurehead for the opposition.

In captivity in the Siberian town of Tobolsk, the deposed Czar Nicholas II and members of his family sit on a platform he himself had built. It was above the greenhouse of the house where they were being held.

The night of July 17

Iakov Iurovskii, the leader of the firing squad that killed the royal family, describes their last moments: "*When the party entered, [I] told the Romanovs that . . . the Execution Committee of the Urals Soviet had decided to shoot them. Nicholas turned his back to the detachment and faced his family. Then, as if collecting himself, he turned around, asking 'What? What?' I rapidly repeated what I had said and ordered the detachment to prepare. Its members had previously been told whom to shoot and to aim directly at the heart, to avoid much blood and to be quickly done. Nicholas said no more. He turned again towards his family. The others shouted some incoherent exclamations. All this lasted a few seconds. Then the shooting began, going on for two or three minutes. I killed Nicholas on the spot.*"

Civil War: Reds Versus Whites

By the middle of 1918, the **Bolshevik** leaders were under siege. Everywhere, their enemies were on the move, and for a time it seemed that the revolution itself might collapse.

Anti-Bolshevik forces, called **Whites** to distinguish them from the **Communist** Reds, attacked on three fronts in what became the **Russian Civil War.** In the south, the **Cossack** revolt had been put down, but the defeated army had regrouped under the leadership of General Anton Denikin, who had taken control after Kornilov was killed. In the east, large parts of Siberia had declared themselves independent of the central government in Moscow. Although various factions, including **democratic socialist** groups, were originally involved, the movement finally came under the command of an ex-**czarist** naval commander, Admiral Alexander Kolchak. In the northwest, a third army under General Nikolai Yudenich grouped in Estonia to prepare an assault on the city of Petrograd.

A visiting group of British officers meets with White Russian forces fighting the Red Army in eastern Russia. Many foreign powers offered money and weapons to the Whites, but not much in the way of troops.

To make matters worse for the Bolsheviks, Russia's wartime **allies** also decided to send troops to fight against the new government. The British and French were angry that the Bolsheviks had pulled out of the war with Germany without consulting them. They were also angry at the Bolsheviks' announcement that they would not repay any of the huge debts that the czar's administration had run up with **Western** bankers and governments. Both countries sent forces north to the White Sea ports, where American troops also landed, and south to the Black Sea. The British ended up holding the port of Archangel for more than a year, while the French seized Odessa. Meanwhile, the Japanese took control of the Pacific port of Vladivostok, at the eastern end of the Trans-Siberian Railroad. They did not return the port to Russia until 1922.

Declaring independence

Taking advantage of the general chaos, the outlying regions of the old czarist empire lost little time in breaking free from Russian rule. Poland had already been lost to the Germans in the course of World War I. Now, Lithuania, Finland, Moldavia, the Ukraine, and the three nations beyond the Caucasus Mountain range—Azerbaijan, Armenia, and Georgia—all declared their independence. Once World War I had ended with a German surrender in November 1918, Poland went further, sending an army to invade Russia. In May 1920, Polish troops even succeeded in capturing the Ukrainian capital of Kiev.

ГРУДЬЮ НА ЗАЩИТУ ПЕТРОГРАДА!

*A **propaganda** poster urges workers and soldiers to defend Petrograd in the civil war. White forces under General Yudenich were driven back from the city in October 1919.*

The Bolsheviks also had problems closer to home. The **left-wing** members of the **Social Revolutionary** party had agreed to enter government with them, but had become increasingly unhappy with their partners. In July 1918 the Social Revolutionaries **assassinated** the German ambassador to Moscow in protest against the **Treaty** of Brest-Litovsk, and then seized the leader of the **Cheka** secret police. Their revolt, though, was more of a protest than a serious attempt to take power and was quickly put down. One month later, another Social Revolutionary, a woman named Fanya Kaplan, tried to assassinate Lenin himself. She shot him in the neck, but he survived.

The Red Terror

The Bolsheviks' answer to the threats was the "Red Terror." The Cheka were given a free hand to arrest and execute all suspected enemies. They seized the chance eagerly. Anyone from a middle-class background was at risk, as were peasants suspected of hoarding grain, or workers unhappy with the long hours they had to work to produce arms to win the war. Some of the victims were unexpected. Lenin's own cousin was executed in Siberia, while in the capital itself a clown named Bim-Bom was shot dead in front of the audience at the Moscow Circus for telling anti-Bolshevik jokes. Prisoners in Cheka jails were subjected to horrifying tortures. Some of the torturers themselves are said to have gone insane as a result of what they saw. No accurate records were kept of the killings, but historians believe that several hundred thousand people were either executed or died in Cheka prison camps, possibly more than in all the battles of the Russian Civil War.

Victory for the Revolution

The threat to the **Bolsheviks** reached a climax in 1919. Early that year, Admiral Kolchak attacked from Siberia, and in July Denikin's southern forces launched a three-pronged drive on Moscow. In October General Yudenich advanced on Petrograd. For a time it seemed that Kolchak and Denikin's forces might link up, putting all southern and eastern Russia in the hands of the **Whites.** Meanwhile, in the far north, a few British troops occupied the ports of Murmansk and Archangel. Later, Great Britain recognized a White government in Archangel.

By the middle of 1920, however, all the threats had been overcome. Kolchak had been captured and executed, and his army fled eastward toward Vladivostok. Denikin's assault had been stopped in two fierce battles in October 1919. Denikin was forced to resign, and his troops retreated back to the **Crimea,** eventually to escape across the Black Sea into **exile** on British and French ships. Yudenich was defeated outside Petrograd and was driven back to Estonia, where his army broke up. Seeing the tide of battle turning, Britain, France, and the other foreign powers first withdrew their own troops and then cut off the supplies of arms and money on which their White **allies** had largely depended.

*Russia during the **Russian Civil War, 1918–20.***

The national uprisings were also stopped. In the north, the Bolsheviks had been forced to recognize the independence of Finland and the Baltic states.

However, the Bolsheviks sent troops to the south to set up **soviet** governments in Azerbaijan, Armenia, and Georgia. The last major threat came from Polish troops, who had invaded the Ukraine in April 1920. The Red Army counterattacked, but when it tried to follow up its early successes by invading Poland itself, it was defeated. At the signing of the **Treaty** of Riga in 1921, Russia agreed to recognize Polish independence.

Why the Reds won

Why did the Bolsheviks win? One reason was the fighting skills of the Red Army, built from scratch by

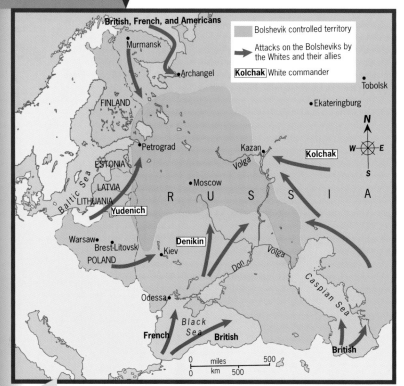

Trotsky from early 1918 on. At its heart were the **Red Guards,** men recruited from the factories who fought alongside pro-Bolshevik soldiers and sailors from the old **czarist** army. It was expanded at first with volunteers, although later others were forced to sign up, with **communists** and workers among the first to be drafted. Eventually all men from the ages of 18 to 40 were called up, creating a force of almost five million men. Although only one in ten of these men were in frontline troops, many more were involved in administration. For battlefield commanders, Trotsky turned to former czarist officers, sending Bolshevik **commissars** to keep an eye on them and using their families as hostages to ensure their loyalty.

Leon Trotsky, the Bolsheviks' military chief, inspects Red Army troops.

Trotsky himself turned out to be an energetic military leader, and he had the advantage of defending a central homeland against enemies who were scattered and out of touch with one another. Probably the main reason why the Bolsheviks won, though, was the attitude of the Whites themselves. To win the war, they needed support within Russia and especially from the peasants, who still made up most of the population. They alone could have provided the invading armies with the food they needed to live on and with fighting men for their ranks. But the peasants never rallied to the White cause. Although they had no love for the Bolsheviks, the revolution had given them land from the old landowners' estates. They feared that the Whites would take these gains away and give the land back to its old owners, which was the last thing they wanted to happen.

Their suspicions were only confirmed by the behavior of the White soldiers, who stole and killed mercilessly in search of supplies. This spread a "White Terror" that was as bad as the the Red Terror, though on a smaller scale. By failing to win over the peasants, the Whites failed to win over Russia, and they paid the price in defeat and exile.

The Last of Lenin

By late 1920, three years of war and revolution had exhausted Russia. Much of the country's rural areas had become virtually self-governing. The peasants in many areas had stopped sending food to the towns because they had no wish to earn money that, because of **inflation,** was literally no longer worth the paper it was printed on. The transportation system had almost ground to a halt, and within the cities many factories had closed down for lack of raw materials to work with. By 1920, industrial production was just one-seventh of its pre-1914 level. Those who could fled to the countryside in search of food. The population of Petrograd dropped from more than two million to just half a million.

War Communism

Driven by the need to support the war, the **Bolsheviks** forced through hard-line economic policies. Under so-called "War **Communism,**" almost all private trade was banned, all industry was brought under state control, and armed bands of **Red Guards** were sent out into the rural areas to collect grain by force. In response, some peasants themselves took up arms, and there were 344 peasant uprisings reported by 1919. Some of the peasant fighters, known as Greens to distinguish themselves from the **Whites** and Reds, ended up controlling entire provinces.

When the war ended in 1920, things seemed to be getting better, but then two years of drought spread famine throughout the land. In some areas, peasants were driven to cannibalism, or eating human flesh, to fight off starvation. In 1921–22, some five million people died of hunger and disease, more than in World War I and the **Russian Civil War** combined. Even formerly loyal supporters of the government now took up the cause of revolt. At the Kronstadt naval base, long a center of Bolshevism, a **mutiny** was brutally put down, and more than 10,000 lives were lost in the process.

The starving children pictured here were victims of the 1921–22 famine. An estimated five million people died of starvation.

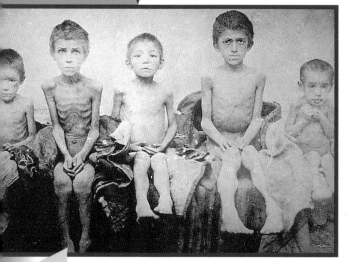

The New Economic Policy

Faced with economic ruin and a rising tide of protest, Lenin decided on a change of direction in 1921. In place of the harsh, state-run approach of War Communism, he brought in the "New Economic Policy," which once more allowed small-scale trading and returned small factories to private ownership. The peasants were to be allowed to sell for profit nine-tenths of the food they

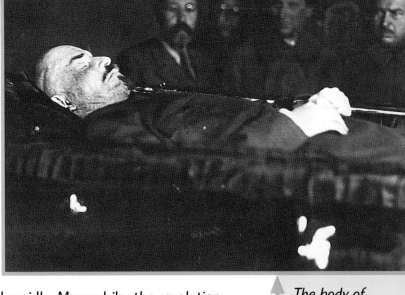

grew, and the state took only the final tenth as a tax. More traditional management and accounting practices were reintroduced, and productive workers were paid higher wages than unproductive ones.

Some **left-wing** Bolsheviks saw the New Economic Policy as a betrayal of their ideals, but the results were dramatic. Agricultural and industrial output both improved rapidly. Meanwhile, the revolution forged ahead in the fields of education and women's rights. Free schooling for all children was introduced, and as a result many people learned how to read

The body of Lenin after his death in January 1924. Half a million people waited in freezing temperatures to view the body.

and write. Women and men were seen as equals according to the law, and divorce and abortion became available on demand. Only in the political field was there no loosening of the reins. In 1921, opposition groups were banned even within the Bolshevik Party itself, which from that year on became known as the **Communist Party.** Hostility to churches

Stepping back to go forward

In a 1921 speech, Lenin explained why he introduced the New Economic Policy: "*We are now retreating, going back as it were, but we are doing this to retreat first and then run forward more vigorously. We retreated on this one condition alone when we introduced out New Economic Policy—so as to begin a more determined offensive after the retreat.*"

and religious leaders also got worse. In February 1922, a **decree** was issued stating that all church valuables should be seized by the state. Several thousand priests were killed in the persecution that followed.

In May 1922, soon after introducing the new program, Lenin had a stroke, setting off a struggle for power within the Communist Party over who should succeed him. When he died in January 1924, he was given a hero's farewell. Half a million people waited in line to pay their last respects. His body was enshrined in a specially built tomb called a mausoleum in Moscow's Red Square. Strangely, his brain was removed and cut into 30,000 slices, supposedly to permit future scientists to study the nature of his genius. The segments are preserved in Moscow to this day. To honor Lenin, Petrograd, the former St. Petersburg, was renamed Leningrad.

Russia and the Outside World

Lenin and his fellow **Bolsheviks** had always believed that the Russian Revolution would be the trigger for other **communist** uprisings around the globe. They believed that their success would mark a **socialist** dawn that would launch a new age in world history.

By the time of Lenin's death, though, it was becoming clear that the rest of the world was not about to follow the Russian example. In 1922, the regions that had failed to establish their independence after the revolution, such as Georgia, Azerbaijan, Armenia, and the Ukraine, were formally grouped together in the Union of **Soviet** Socialist Republics, known as the USSR or **Soviet Union.** As for the rest of the world, Lenin's eventual successor Joseph Stalin, himself a Georgian, came to the conclusion that for the time being the nation should stop trying to export **communism.** Instead, it should concentrate on a policy known as "building socialism in one country," which in Russia's case would mean building up the nation's economic and military strength.

Stalin seizes power

Stalin had not been Lenin's choice as his successor—in a secret memo, he had called him too coarse and intolerant—and Stalin soon lived up to Lenin's worst fears. Through clever political maneuvering, he managed to gain total control of the **Communist Party** and then set about eliminating all his rivals. Trotsky was driven into **exile** in 1929 and was **assassinated** in Mexico on Stalin's orders eleven years later. By that time, most of the old Bolshevik leadership had been killed following a series of **show trials** in which the accused were forced to confess to unlikely charges of treason or conspiracy and then executed.

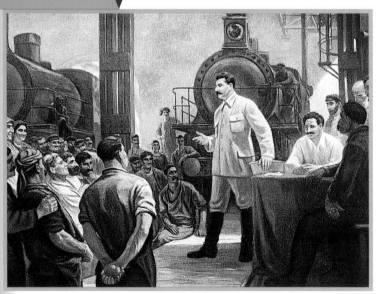

This painting shows Stalin in 1926 giving a speech to workers at a train engine factory. Stalin was determined to industrialize the USSR. His tough policies led to a dramatic increase in industrial production in the years before World War Two.

With all opposition frightened into silence by his reign of terror, Stalin ruled as a **dictator,** using his powers to push through **radical** changes in Russian society. He succeeded in **industrializing** the USSR through a series of five-year plans. He did away with the old village **communes** throughout the country and forced the peasants to work as employees on **collective farms** run as factories were. Millions died trying to resist this policy.

Stalin lived in constant fear of attack, not just from enemies within Russia but also from foreign powers. In the 1930s, he had good reason to fear the intentions of **Nazi** Germany. Its leader, Adolf Hitler, was committed to destroying Soviet communism. After making a temporary alliance of convenience with his archenemy in the Nazi-Soviet Pact of 1939, designed to buy time to build up the Red Army, Stalin had to cope with a full-scale German invasion from 1941 on.

The Soviet Union during the Cold War years.

The coming of the Cold War

For four years during World War II, the USSR fought for its life, helped by the United States and Great Britain, which were its partners in the war against Nazism. Victory in 1945, however, soon gave way to the development of tensions between these three powers. Stalin's successful attempts to force communist rule on the countries adjoining the Soviet Union's western borders, in particular Poland, Czechoslovakia, and Hungary, raised fears that the nation had moved from "socialism in one country" to nothing less than a drive for world domination. The result was the **Cold War,** which for the next 45 years effectively split much of the world into hostile communist and anticommunist camps. To its enemies, the new Russian empire was more dictatorial and repressive than anything known in the time of the **czars.**

In March 1946, Great Britain's war leader Winston Churchill spoke of a new division of Europe. "*A shadow has fallen across the scenes so lately lighted by the Allied victory. From Stettin on the Baltic to Trieste on the Adriatic an iron curtain has descended across the continent . . .*" Nowhere was this more evident than in the divided city of Berlin, Germany, where the USSR built a wall to stop East Berliners from escaping to the West.

The Soviet Collapse

U.S. President Kennedy (right) and Soviet Premier Khrushchev (left) are pictured here in Vienna, Austria, in 1961. A year later, their countries almost went to war when the United States discovered Russian nuclear missiles on the island of Cuba.

The **Cold War** world that emerged out of World War II was one based on fear on both sides. The **Western Allies** feared the spread of **communism** around the world. Stalin feared the Allies' policy of containment, which looked to him like an attempt to keep Russia down, much in the same way that he believed the Allies had tried to stamp out **Bolshevism** by their interventions in the **Russian Civil War.** The alarm on each side was increased by the knowledge that the other had nuclear weapons that could destroy entire nations, if not the world itself.

For more than 40 years, the Cold War blew hot and cold as global crises came and went. There was a temporary improvement in relations after the death of Stalin in 1953. The subsequent Russian campaign of "destalinization" aimed at exposing some of the excesses of his rule. The climate chilled again in 1956, when the Russians sent troops to stop a popular uprising against **Soviet** rule in Hungary. The Cold War reached an all-time low in 1962, when U.S. President

John F. Kennedy received evidence that Russian missiles were being sent to Cuba, a communist-run island situated just 90 miles (145 kilometers) south of the state of Florida. For a few days, the threat of nuclear war loomed. At the last moment, Russian Premier Nikita Khruschev agreed to withdraw the weapons, and the world breathed a collective sigh of relief.

Costs of the Cold War

Meanwhile, the pressure of nonstop military rivalry with the United States was having a damaging effect on the USSR. The Bolsheviks had believed that a communist system in which people worked for the benefit of society as a whole would quickly outstrip a **capitalist** one. In practice, though, it was the capitalist United States that provided the best standard of living for its workers and delivered the fastest economic growth. It also proved better at delivering the goods that people wanted. The much smaller Russian economy was held back by the strain of heavy and continued spending on arms. Meanwhile, the high hopes of an equal society that had buoyed up the Bolsheviks had slowly drained away. Ordinary Russians saw that **Communist Party bureaucrats** enjoyed a high standard of living while they still had difficulty getting the basic necessities in life.

The final straw came in Afghanistan, where the Red Army intervened in 1979 to force a pro-Russian ruler on a passionately Muslim people. The war lasted nine years, draining the **Soviet Union's** human and material resources. At the same time, under President Ronald Reagan, the United States was spending military funds on an expensive new strategic defense program, dubbed "Star Wars" by reporters. The USSR simply could not keep up.

Changing the system

When a new, dynamic leader, Mikhail Gorbachev, came to power in Moscow in 1985, he saw the need for change. Preaching the doctrine of *glasnost,* or openness, and *perestroika,* which means economic restructuring, he turned his back on almost 70 years of centralized planning by the state. At the same time, he abandoned the arms race with the West, driving forward a large-scale program of weapons cuts. Among the first to benefit from the new climate of freedom were the USSR's unwilling partners in eastern Europe, which took the opportunity to declare their independence from Soviet control. The new era was symbolized by the breaking down, in 1989, of the Berlin Wall. East and West Germany were reunited. Poland, Hungary, Czechoslovakia, Lithuania, Romania, and Bulgaria all elected their own governments in the early years of the 1990s.

By December 1991, the USSR for the most part had ceased to exist. Some regions that were part of the USSR gained independence, and others started demanding the same. Russia, Ukraine, and Belarus all agreed to join a new grouping called the Commonwealth of Independent States. Later, so did most of the regions that had been part of the USSR. Russia held its first entirely free elections, and Boris Yeltsin was voted president.

Russia finally turned its back on the communist past. Symbolic of this break with the past, Leningrad was renamed St. Petersburg. Suddenly, the events of 1917 appeared in a new light. The events had **radically** changed Russia and the course of world history. They had not, however, set Russia's course forever, as the Bolsheviks had thought they would.

While East German border guards look on passively, a West German demonstrator uses a sledgehammer to hit the Berlin Wall. The demolition of the wall in 1989 symbolically marked the end of the Soviet era in eastern Europe.

The Legacy of the Russian Revolution

The people who made the Russian Revolution hoped that it would prove to be a model for all humankind. The **Bolsheviks** dreamed of ushering in an age of social justice and universal harmony around the globe. That hope quickly proved to be unfounded. Under Joseph Stalin, Russia experienced terrible injustices and brutal **dictatorship.** In the **Cold War** years, the world became more deeply divided, and on one occasion came close to a nuclear war.

The gulags

Those dreaming of a freer and more open country were also disappointed. Criticism of the **communist** system in the USSR was not allowed, and opponents of the regime were sent off to forced-labor camps run by a sinister organization called the gulag. It has been estimated that up to six million **political prisoners** were held in captivity at any one time. During Stalin's dictatorship, many people in the gulags died from overwork and starvation. After Stalin's death, some were released, and conditions in these prison camps did improve.

Russia's progress from communism to democracy has not been easy. During the late 1990s, people were forced to wait in line for basic products, and rising prices caused particular hardship among elderly people.

With the abandonment of **communism** in Russia in the 1990s, it became easy to see the revolution as no more than a terrible mistake. Yet the events of 1917 had left a positive mark on Russia. The society that emerged from the chaos of the revolution was a much more equal one than anything that had been known under the **czars.** The Russian people were also better educated.

Mandatory schooling had lessened the hold of superstition and outdated ideas on the minds of the people of this vast country.

Improvements for women

The status of women had also improved. In czarist times, women were expected to do backbreaking work in the fields, but they had few rights. Under the **Soviet** regime, women received equality according to the law, and they were able to do work that had previously been reserved for only men. This proved to be a heavy burden for some women, because in some cases they were still expected to carry out more traditional tasks as well.

Economically by the 1990s, Russia had been transformed from a largely agricultural land to one with a huge, though aging, industrial base. It also showed it was capable of cutting-edge technological advancement in certain selected fields, notably space research. Some of these changes were starting even under the last czar, but the revolution speeded them up.

The global impact

The Russian experiment changed the outside world, too. Revolutionaries in other countries took inspiration from Lenin's success. One revolutionary leader, Mao Zedong, turned China into a communist nation in 1949. In the **West,** too, many idealistic individuals fell under the spell of communism in the early years. Support for the Russian variety of communism fell away fast from the 1950s onward, though, after the facts of Stalin's tyranny and of Soviet oppression in Eastern Europe became widely known. In the Western **democracies,** fear of a communist takeover was an often unspoken influence leading governments to insist on fairer treatment for their own workers. It is perhaps no coincidence that since the collapse of the **Soviet Union** the gap between rich and poor has begun to increase once more around the world.

Although the Cold War divided some nations, it brought others closer together. Fear of a spread of communism helped create support for Western alliances such as the North Atlantic **Treaty** Organization, or NATO, formed in 1949. With a communist enemy on their doorstep, Western European economies drew closer together, forming the European Economic Community, or EEC, now known as the European Union, or EU.

Sadly, the high ideals that inspired the Russian Revolution were let down by the undemocratic means used to bring them about. Russia in 1917 proved too deeply divided for change to come about through common consent. Instead, it came through confrontation and bloodshed. The results are being felt around the world to this day.

With the collapse of communism in the Soviet Union, China was left as the world's biggest communist power, with well over one billion people.

Timeline

1861	**Czar** Alexander II frees the serfs
1881	Alexander II **assassinated** by terrorists; he is succeeded by Alexander III
1894	Nicholas II becomes czar
1898	**Social Democratic** Party founded
1902	**Social Revolutionary** Party founded
1903	Trans-Siberian Railroad completed
	Social Democrats split between **Bolsheviks** and **Mensheviks**
1904	Russo-Japanese War breaks out
	V. K. Plehve, minister of the interior, assassinated
1905	"Bloody Sunday" massacre of demonstrators in St. Petersburg
	Russia defeated by Japanese in battles of Mukden and Tsushima
	Czar issues "October Manifesto," promising constitutional change
1906	"Fundamental Laws" reaffirm **autocracy** (one-man rule)
	First **Duma** (parliament) called, to be dissolved after two months
	Peter Stolypin becomes prime minister
1907	New, less **democratic** Duma elected
1911	Stolypin assassinated
1914	Outbreak of World War I
	Russia, **allied** with Britain and France, declares war on Germany and Austria-Hungary
	Russia defeated at Tannenberg and the Masurian Lakes
1915	Czar Nicholas takes charge of army as commander-in-chief
1916	Rasputin murdered by **aristocratic** conspirators
1917	March: First revolution forces czar to abdicate (give up power)
	Provisional Government set up to organize democratic elections
	Russian army suffers new defeats in Austria-Hungary
	In the "July days" riots, Bolsheviks try unsuccessfully to seize power
	Alexander Kerensky takes over as leader of Provisional Government
	September: General Lavr Kornilov stages an unsuccessful military coup
	November: Bolsheviks take over Petrograd (St. Petersburg) and proclaim Russian Revolution
1918	January: Bolsheviks dissolve the **Constituent Assembly**
	Russia makes peace with Germany at **Treaty** of Brest-Litovsk
	July: Nicholas II and his family murdered
	Civil war breaks out between Red and White forces
1920	Red forces victorious in the civil war
1921	Lenin announces "New Economic Policy," allowing some private trade
	Famine spreads across Russia
1924	Death of Lenin starts power struggle in Bolshevik Party
1927	Stalin emerges as Russia's unchallenged leader
1939	Nazi-Soviet Pact signed by Germany and Russia

1941	German armies invade Russia
1945	Russia emerges victorious from World War II but with an estimated 26 million citizens dead
	Start of **Cold War**
1953	Death of Stalin
1961	Berlin Wall divides East from West Berlin
1962	Cuban missile crisis
1985	Mikhail Gorbachev becomes leader of USSR and announces new policy of glasnost (openness)
1989	Berlin Wall demolished, signaling end of Cold War
1991	Boris Yeltsin becomes president of a noncommunist Russia
	USSR broken up, to be replaced by Commonwealth of Independent States

Further Reading

Dowswell, Paul. *Weapons and Technology of World War I.* Chicago: Heinemann Library, 2002.

Edwards, Judith. *Lenin and the Russian Revolution in World History.* Berkeley Heights, N.J.: Enslow Publishers, 2001.

Taylor, David. *The Cold War.* Chicago: Heinemann Library, 2001.

Taylor, David. *Key Battles of World War I.* Chicago: Heinemann Library, 2001.

Willoughby, Susan. *The Russian Revolution.* Chicago: Heinemann Library, 1997.

Glossary

allies friendly countries who agree to support one another. The Allies were a group of countries that fought together in World Wars I and II and were on the side of Great Britain, France, and the United States.

aristocracy people who have high positions in society, which they have usually inherited from their parents

assassination murder for political reasons

Austria-Hungary Central European empire, broken up after World War I

autocracy one-man rule

Bolsheviks Social Democrats who followed Vladimir Lenin

bureaucrat privileged officeholder

Cadets members of the Constitutional Democratic party who support parliamentary rule

capitalist describing an economic system in which factories and businesses are owned by private individuals for their own profit and in which government control over those businesses and industries is minimal

censorship banning of information for political or other reasons

Cheka Bolshevik secret police

Cold War 45-year hostilities between capitalist countries, led by the United States, and the communist bloc, led by the Soviet Union, after World War II

collective farm farm in which land, tools, and other property are owned in common rather than by individual families

commissar Communist Party official

commune community in which members share duties, responsibilities, and property

communism political system where private ownership has been abolished and where factories and industries are run by the state for the benefit of all. A follower of communism is called a communist.

Communist Party name used by the Bolshevik Party from the 1920s on

Constituent Assembly assembly elected in 1918 to work out a new constitution for Russia. It was never able to do this because it was broken up by the Bolsheviks.

Cossacks peasant fighters from the southern Ukraine

counterrevolutionary person opposed to and who fights against the forces of a revolution

coup armed takeover of power

Crimea peninsula in south Russia extending into the Black Sea

czar type of ruler Russia had before the Russian Revolution

decree order or command

democracy method of governing in which the people of the country choose their leaders in elections

dictator person who has complete control of a country. A country run by a dictator is a dictatorship.

diplomacy solving problems through discussions with other nations

Duma name of Russia's parliament called by the czar after 1905

emancipation to set free, usually from some sort of slavery

exile being sent away from one's own country or region and not being allowed to return

gentry upper or ruling class of people in society

human rights right of everyone to live without injustice, persecution, or discrimination

inflation widespread rise in prices

left-wing in political terms, leaning toward a socialist or communist viewpoint

Marxist follower of the communist philosophy of the German philosopher Karl Marx

Mensheviks Social Democrats who were opposed to Vladimir Lenin

militia army often made up of civilians

mobilization calling up of an army for war

mutiny revolt against someone in charge, usually in the army or navy

nationalize to bring under the control of a national government

Nazi member of the right-wing National Socialist Party in Germany during Adolf Hitler's time

nobleman person of high class or rank who also usually was a landowner

patriotism strong feelings of loyalty for one's country

political prisoner person who is imprisoned because of their political beliefs

propaganda information spread for political purposes

Provisional Government temporary government set up in Russia to call for parliamentary elections after the czar was forced to step down in 1917

radicals people who want to make extreme changes. A radical change is a extreme change.

Red Guards Bolshevik military force of armed workers

right-wing in political terms, leaning toward a more conservative or monarchist viewpoint

Russian Civil War war fought between communists, called Reds, and supporters of Czar Nicholas II, called Whites, from 1918 to 1921. The war was won by the Reds.

serf peasant who had to serve one landowner for his or her entire life

show trial trial held for propaganda purposes

socialism political system in which wealth is shared equally and some of the main industries are run by the government. Someone who supports this system is called a socialist.

Social Democrat member of a Russian political movement inspired by the views of the German philosopher Karl Marx

Social Revolutionary member of a Russian revolutionary movement that was focused on getting the peasants of Russia to revolt against the government

soviet workers' or peasants' council. This word also became part of the name of the Union of Soviet Socialist Republics (USSR), one of the most powerful communist nations in the world until its collapse in 1990.

Soviet Union another name for the USSR

stock market place where stocks and shares are traded

strike when people refuse to work as a way of making a protest

trade unions organized groups of workers usually set up to help improve both pay and working conditions

treaty agreement between countries

West, Western political, rather than geographical, name for the industrialized countries of western Europe, North America, Australia, and New Zealand

Whites opponents of the Reds (Bolsheviks) in the Russian Civil War

working class people who work for wages, often doing manual or industrial work

Index